You've Got Quirks
And You're Wonderful

Written by Kristin A. Sherry

&

Illustrated by Mel Schroeder

This Book Belongs to:

_____

To Xander for embracing my quirks with grace,
and to Nicole for suggesting I write this book.

You have a surprise inside you.
Everyone who has ever lived has this surprise too.
But some people don't know it.
Would you like to know what that surprise is?

Before sharing the surprise, I'd like you to meet some special people.
Their stories will make the wait worth it, and maybe they'll help you discover the surprise.

I am awesome

I am Confident

I am perfect how I am

I AM GRATEFUL

I am proud of myself

Winnie

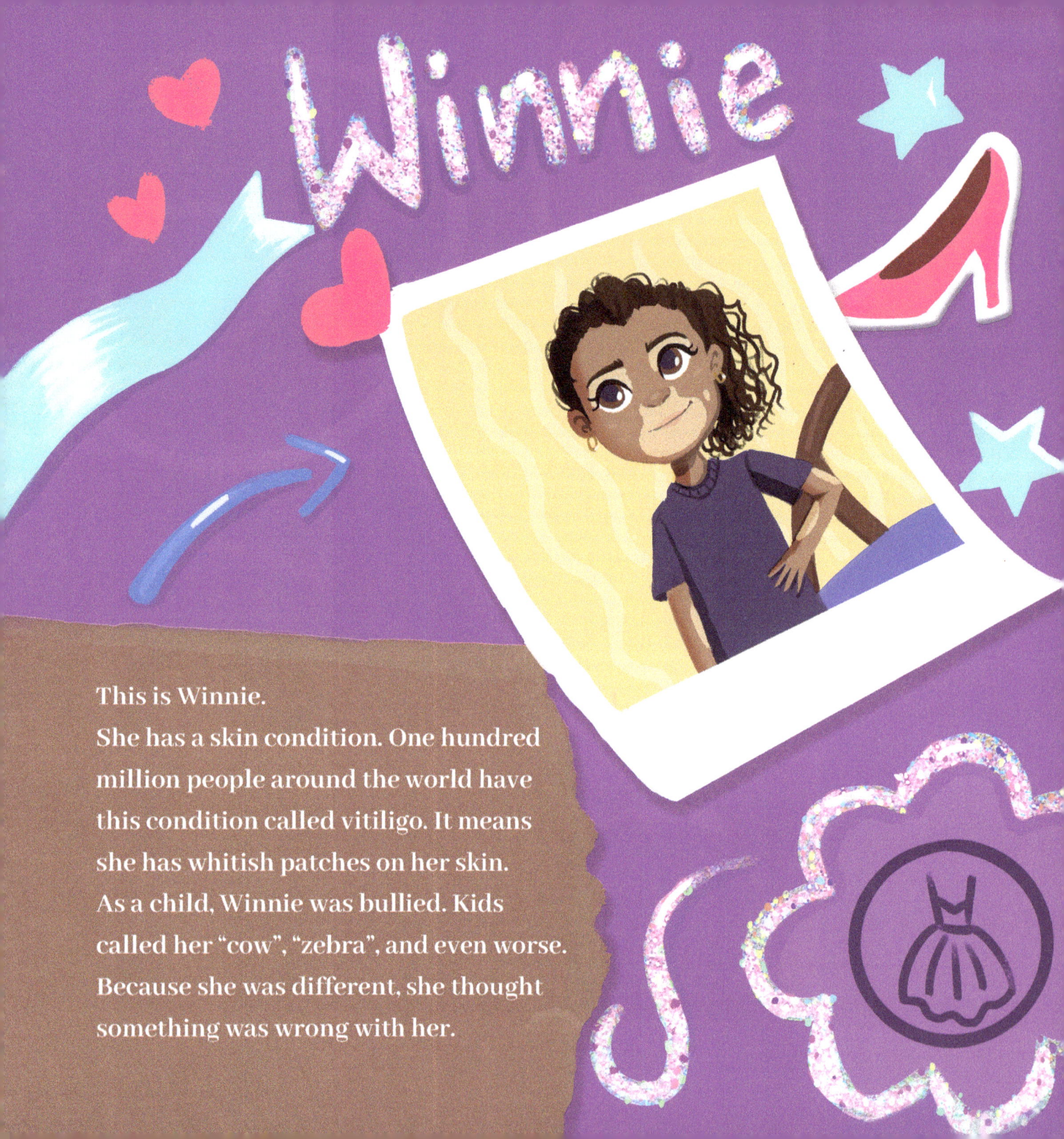

This is Winnie.
She has a skin condition. One hundred million people around the world have this condition called vitiligo. It means she has whitish patches on her skin. As a child, Winnie was bullied. Kids called her "cow", "zebra", and even worse. Because she was different, she thought something was wrong with her.

Today, Winnie is a model. Her picture has shown up on the covers of magazines, and top designers picked her to wear their clothes on fashion show runways.

Winnie says, "There is beauty in everything. I learned to love who I am despite what anyone would say about me. This gave me the courage to really stand up to anyone or any obstacle in my life."

Jake

This is Jake.

He has Tourette's Syndrome.

At five years old, Jake started to have tics, which are movements and sounds a person can't control that repeat over and over, like blinking and shoulder shrugging.

Kids would stare at Jake when his tics began. They mocked him, blinking quickly and saying, "Guess who I am?"

Jake worried his friends would be embarrassed to be near him.

As Jake got older, he chose to embrace Tourette's as part of who he is. He started sharing his story. When he did, other people didn't feel alone.

Jake was amazed at how supportive people were!

He began speaking on social media, at events, and companies, and he met other people with Tourette's, too. Jake's story has reached hundreds of thousands of people. Jake says, "Once I accepted myself for who I was, I was no longer ashamed. I was no longer afraid to be ME!"

ANNE

be kind

This is Anne.
She grew up poor.
Anne's mother often brought home garbage bags of hand-me-down clothes from other families for Anne and her siblings to wear.
Some girls didn't want to be friends with Anne because of how she looked, dressed, and where she lived.
This made Anne feel mad and sad.
Anne often wished she could live in a nice house, in a nice neighborhood, and have new clothes.

As an adult, Anne has a home of her own and new clothes, but she has learned "things" don't define you.

Though Anne's mother couldn't buy her nice things, she gave Anne something better. She taught her to work hard, be kind, and not judge others. These lessons have helped Anne live a happy life.

She says, "Kids can be mean. It's not a reflection of who you are. Hold your head high. Just because your home situation is different from others doesn't mean YOU are not awesome!"

This is LeRon.
He has a stutter. Stuttering is a speech disorder and causes a person to repeat sounds or words. Someone who stutters knows exactly what he or she would like to say, but has trouble saying it. People made fun of LeRon when he stuttered because it took him a long time to say something. They would stare and laugh at him as he struggled to speak.

Now, LeRon understands his stutter is a part of him, but it is not who he is! He doesn't try to hide his stutter and openly tells people he has one. LeRon is an author and speaks on stages around the world. He also gives talks to other people who stutter, encouraging them not to give up.

LeRon says, "Having a stutter is hard, and kids can be mean, but you can believe in yourself. Do not beat yourself up; your stutter is a small part of you!"

CHRISTINA

This is Christina.

She has Autism Spectrum Disorder (ASD). Kids with ASD have brains that work differently. They might find it hard to talk with others, or have feelings too big for them to handle. Because they focus deeply on their interests, they often don't fit in.

Growing up, Christina had a hard time relating to kids. She often sat alone, thinking about why grass grows and how clouds move. She loved to answer the teacher's questions, so she was called a "dork" and teased almost daily. She believed she couldn't be herself.

SHINE BRIGHT

Christina has discovered the gifts of ASD. She is smart, sees patterns others don't see, and thinks in pictures! People with ASD are often fair and honest, which makes them easy to trust.

Today, Christina runs her own business. Because she thinks and sees the world differently, her special abilities help her customers tell powerful stories to grow their businesses.

Christina says, "There are people who will appreciate you for exactly who you are. Don't ever hide yourself for the sake of other people. Shine bright."

This is Miguel.
He was a sensitive child who felt emotions deeply. We call this having empathy.
Miguel was told boys don't cry. He was called weak, emotional, and a crybaby.
Sometimes people would make fun of Miguel by calling him a girl and telling him to "be a man."

Now, empathy is Miguel's superpower. He understands people say mean things because they are hurting inside. We can choose to be kind in return because we realize their words aren't really about us. Miguel has created his life based on love and values and helps others do the same.

Empathy has made Miguel the father he dreamed of being, full of love and understanding.

Miguel says, "You can choose to lead by example to help create a more understanding and caring world."

Diana

This is Diana.
She often snorts when she laughs.
One day, a snort-filled laugh sent a mucus bubble out of Diana's nose in front of the other kids! They imitated her laugh and called her "bubble girl."
Diana began to hide her laugh and her smile.

Today, Diana is an actress and comedian. She has performed her comedy show to sold out audiences. Diana also hosts a live interview and podcast called "The SnortCast," bringing funny people around the world together with laughter.

People now laugh with Diana, not at her.

Diana says, "Share your quirks with the important people in your life. They can protect and support you and share their quirks with you, too."

Nick

This is Nick.
He was born without arms or legs. Kids at school picked on Nick every day, calling him "ugly" and "weird."
Nick thought he would never get married, never have children, and never live a happy life.

Today, Nick is married with four children. He has written books and travels the world speaking to huge crowds with his message of hope.

Even without arms or legs, Nick has gone scuba diving, played football, and surfed. Nick says, "Your attitude will determine how high you will fly in life!"

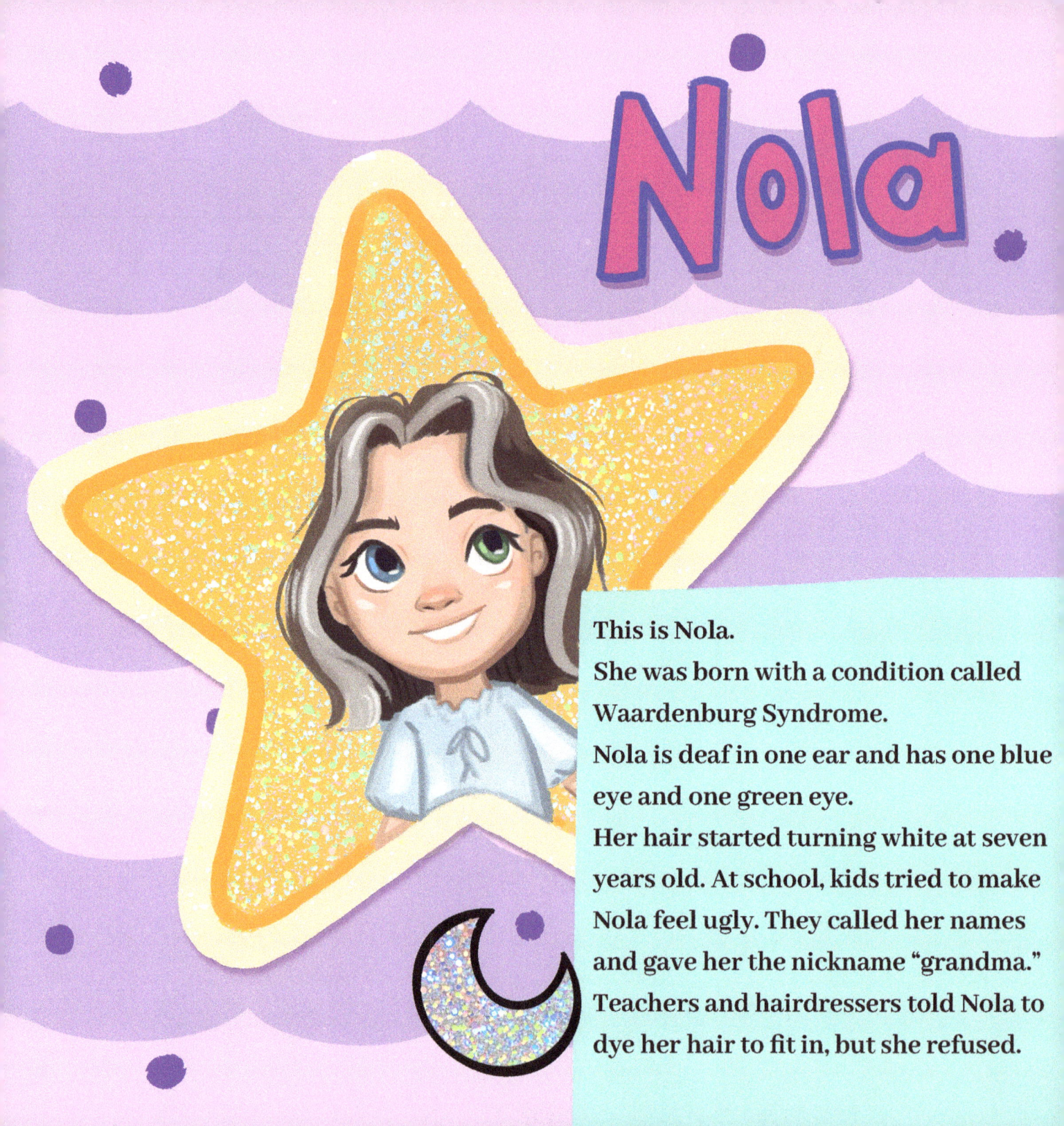

Nola

This is Nola.
She was born with a condition called Waardenburg Syndrome.
Nola is deaf in one ear and has one blue eye and one green eye.
Her hair started turning white at seven years old. At school, kids tried to make Nola feel ugly. They called her names and gave her the nickname "grandma." Teachers and hairdressers told Nola to dye her hair to fit in, but she refused.

When Nola was little, being different was hard.
In time, she began to embrace what made her unique. Nola learned two important lessons she wants to share.
Nola says, "Tune out negativity and be comfortable with being different!"

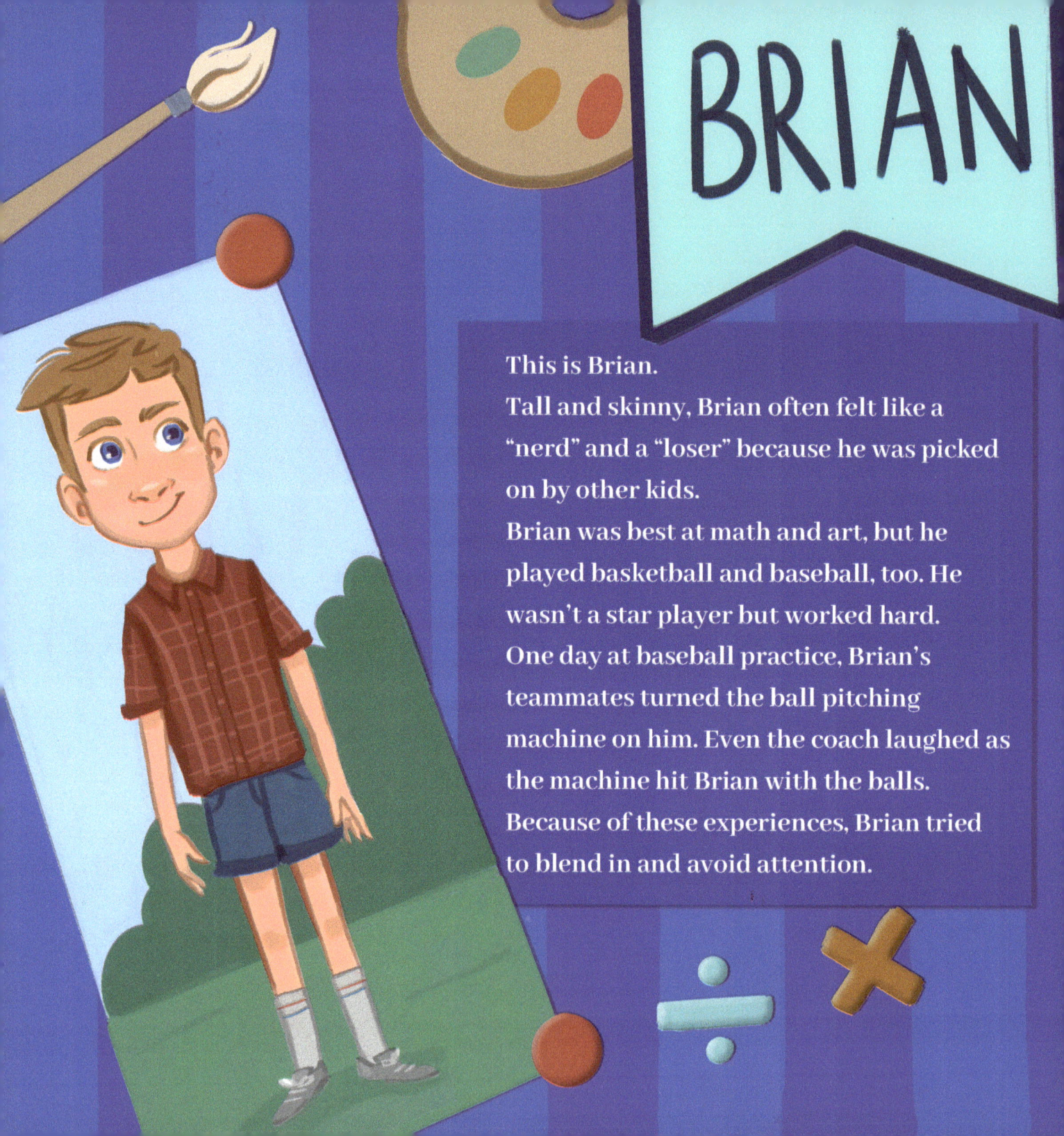

BRIAN

This is Brian.

Tall and skinny, Brian often felt like a "nerd" and a "loser" because he was picked on by other kids.

Brian was best at math and art, but he played basketball and baseball, too. He wasn't a star player but worked hard. One day at baseball practice, Brian's teammates turned the ball pitching machine on him. Even the coach laughed as the machine hit Brian with the balls. Because of these experiences, Brian tried to blend in and avoid attention.

Now, Brian stands up for the underdogs who aren't seen as winners. He teaches his sons to stand up for others, too.

Brian chose to turn his experiences into a positive by being a kind and caring leader. He is a Chief Master Sergeant, the highest enlisted rank, in the U.S. Air Force.

Brian says, "Both good and bad experiences in our lives can teach us how to be a better person."

ERICA

This is Erica.

She is a curvy Spanish girl who was a little overweight.

As a child, Erica was bullied. Kids called her "gordita," which is Spanish for "little fat girl." They poked her stomach and laughed at her.

Because she was different, she was embarrassed to go to pool parties and always wondered if people would laugh at her.

Today, Erica is a teacher. She helps people learn about healthy food and fun ways to exercise. Erica always reminds her students to be nice to others, no matter what they look like. She tells them that curves don't matter. Kind people are the prettiest.
Erica says, "I am both curvy and kind, beautiful in my own way, just like you."

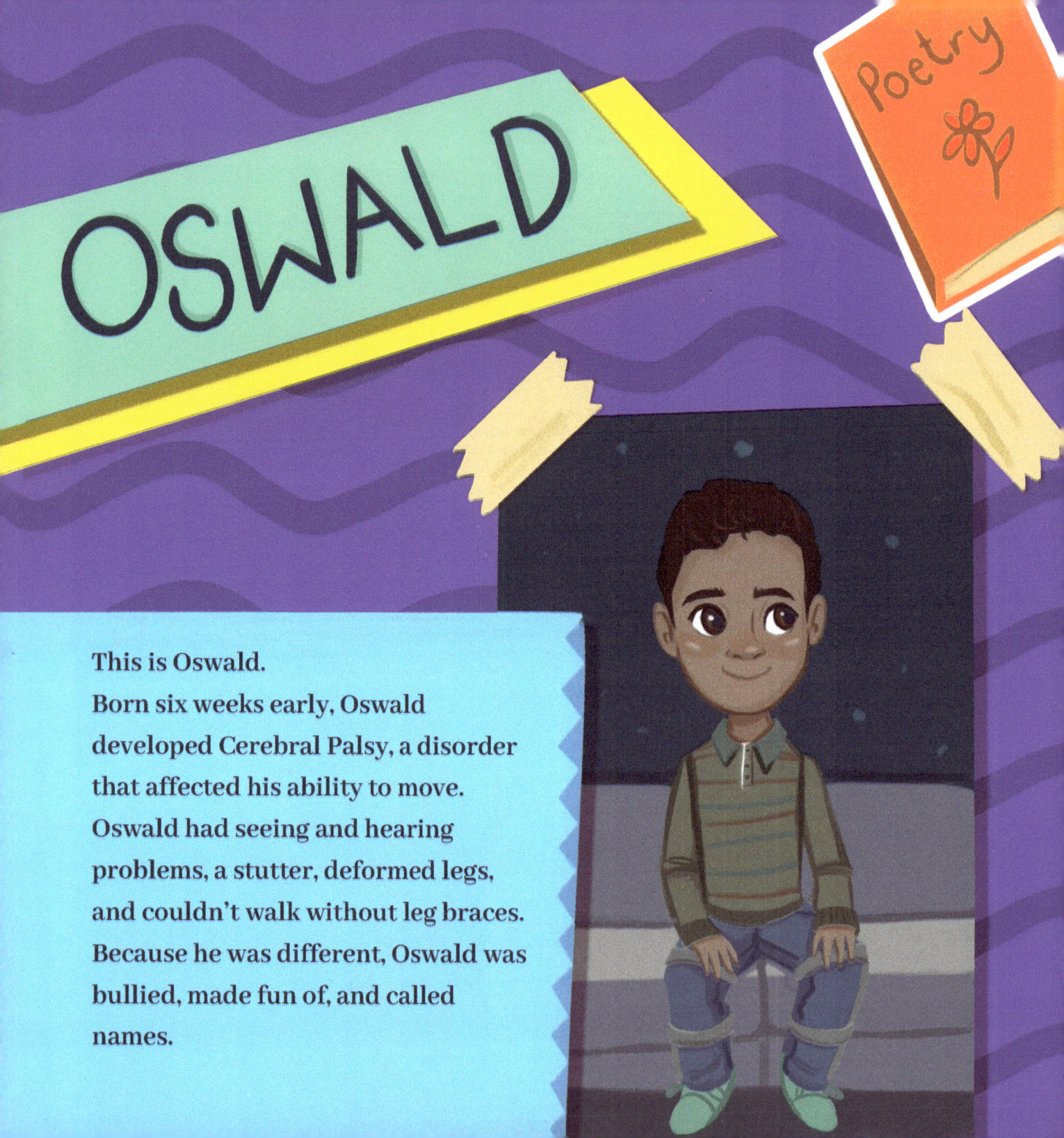

OSWALD

This is Oswald.
Born six weeks early, Oswald developed Cerebral Palsy, a disorder that affected his ability to move. Oswald had seeing and hearing problems, a stutter, deformed legs, and couldn't walk without leg braces. Because he was different, Oswald was bullied, made fun of, and called names.

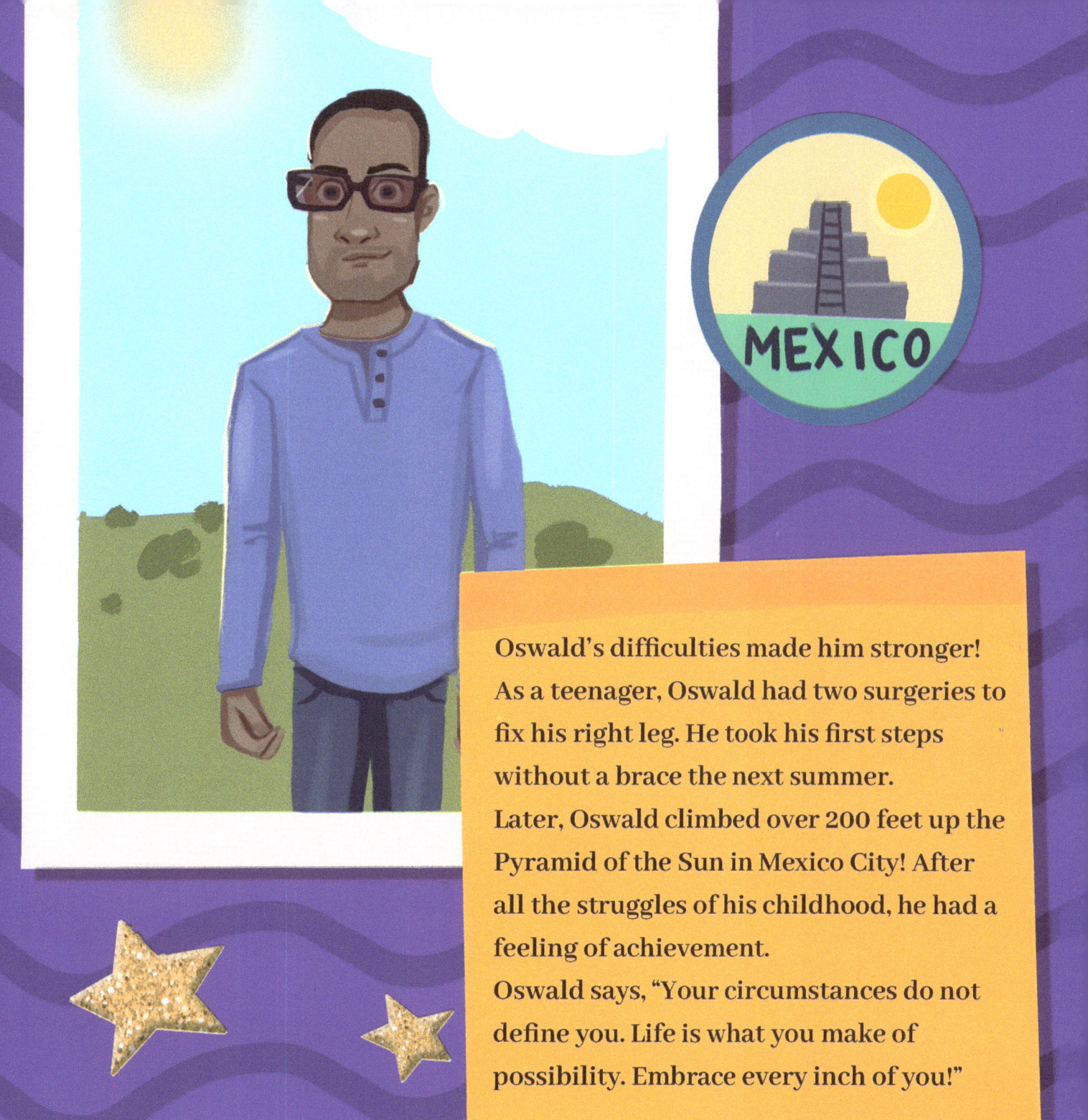

MEXICO

Oswald's difficulties made him stronger! As a teenager, Oswald had two surgeries to fix his right leg. He took his first steps without a brace the next summer.

Later, Oswald climbed over 200 feet up the Pyramid of the Sun in Mexico City! After all the struggles of his childhood, he had a feeling of achievement.

Oswald says, "Your circumstances do not define you. Life is what you make of possibility. Embrace every inch of you!"

Now that you've met my friends, have you guessed the surprise?
The surprise is...

WE ALL HAVE QUIRKS!

Quirks people have can be big or quite small.
Maybe you're extremely short or somewhat tall.
You bite your fingernails or suck your thumb.
Maybe you're teased, and some call you dumb.
You have freckles, strange birthmarks, or even a scar.
Maybe you talk funny or get sick in the car!
But whatever your quirks, embrace who you are.
Don't let them stop you, and you too can go far!

Ideas for Discussion

1. Teach children how they can respond when they meet someone with a visible or noticeable "quirk."

– Address a child's curiosity about differences openly and honestly, offering short, to the point answers to help your child see that person is a person just like anyone else.

– Use positive terms like, "I see you noticing the boy in the wheelchair. A wheelchair helps him get around, like your legs help you," instead of saying, "He can't walk."

– Encourage the child to talk to the person. For example, ask how a wheelchair helps them or how they deal with their challenges.

– Use respectful rather than derogatory words, and avoid using a disability to describe a person. Instead of "autistic child" you can say, "a child on the autism spectrum."

– Explain each child is unique, but also emphasize similarities between your child and the other person.

– Teach empathy by explaining everyone has strengths and weaknesses.

– Encourage children to look beyond a "quirk" or label and get to know a person, talking to her, playing with her, and asking about her interests.

– Explain children with visible "quirks" want to be treated the same as other people.

– Directly discuss and condemn bullying.

– Teach children to respect medical devices such as canes and wheelchairs. Explain these devices are not toys.

2. People sometimes tease others to take attention from their own insecurities and hurts.
- Talk to children about how common and normal it is to struggle with confidence.
- Discuss how people might treat others, if they aren't confident, and why they may act this way.
- Share a personal story.

3. We can practice not allowing other people to control our emotions.
- When we allow people to upset us, we hand over control of our feelings to another –Discuss ideas to practice making this choice.

4. Things we were insecure about as kids often don't matter as adults.
- Share an example of something you were embarrassed about when you were younger that is now insignificant to you.

5. Encourage children to share a quirk they are embarrassed about.
- Acknowledge how he or she is feeling and offer support and appreciation.
- Share a personal story.

6. When we speak openly about a quirk, it takes away a bully's power.

Example:

Davis had a stutter. On the first day of school, the teacher asked students their preferred name. Davis responded, "I go by Davis, or Dave, and some people call me 'Duva, Duva, Davis.'" No one teased Davis after that because he embraced the humor in his stutter.

About the Author

Kristin A. Sherry is an award-winning, bestselling author. She is the creator of the YouMap® Career Profile and managing partner of YouMap LLC, which certifies coaches to change lives with YouMap®.

You've Got Quirks is Kristin's fifth children's book. Others include *Mom's Choice Awards®* Gold recipients *You've Got Gifts!* (2021 *Maxy Awards* Children's Book of the Year finalist), *You've Got Values!*, *You've Got Skills!*, and *You've Got Personality!*, which help children build confidence through self-awareness.

Kristin is also the author of career and self-development books *YouMap, Your Team Loves Mondays…Right?*, and *Maximize 365: A Year of Actionable Tips to Transform Your Life*, an Indie Book Award Motivational Book of the Year winner.

Kristin and her husband Xander reside with their children in North Carolina.

www.kristinsherry.info.

About the Illustrator

Mel Schroeder is a freelance children's book illustrator. She studied Animation and Digital Arts and graduated in 2014. In addition to illustrating, Mel teaches college-level concept art classes, and works on various illustration and children's book collaborations, as well as covers, and editorial pieces. Her main projects involve fantasy, childhood, and nature.

Follow Mel on Instagram at @melschroederart,
and visit her website at melschroederart.com.

Black Rose writing™

© 2022 Kristin A. Sherry
© 2022 Illustrations by Mel Schroeder

All rights reserved. No part of this book may be reproduced, stored in a retrieval system or transmitted in any form or by any means without the prior written permission of the publishers, except by a reviewer who may quote brief passages in a review to be printed in a newspaper, magazine or journal.

The final approval for this literary material is granted by the author.

First printing/ First Hardcover

This is a work of fiction. Names, characters, businesses, places, events and incidents are either the products of the author's imagination or used in a fictitious manner. Any resemblance to actual persons, living or dead, or actual events is purely coincidental.

ISBN: 978-1-68433-898-6 (Paperback)
978-1-68433-899-3 (Hardcover)
PUBLISHED BY BLACK ROSE WRITING
www.blackrosewriting.com

Printed in the United States of America

www.ingramcontent.com/pod-product-compliance
Lightning Source LLC
Chambersburg PA
CBHW061115070526
44583CB00027B/3306